How to ~~Beat~~

Haters

Understanding and Handling Jerks, Manipulators and Bullies

Book Ten of the Cyrus Kirkpatrick Lifestyle Design Series

By Cyrus Kirkpatrick of www.cyruskirkpatrick.com

(Freedom Based Work Strategies and Adventure Travel)

Copyright 2015 C.K. Media Enterprises L.L.C, All Rights Reserved

**Cyrus Kirkpatrick
Lifestyle Design Series**

Special Message: Thank you for your purchase of "How to Deal With Haters". I try to maintain quality in the production of my books. This is because of a disappointing trend in the self-publishing world where cheap, outsourced books are mass-produced by marketing firms. They are often unedited or with poor grammar, yet are passed off as real products. It's up to both readers and writers to keep the market quality and spam-free.

Free Supplemental Booklet: Right now you can check out www.cyruskirkpatrick.com/subscribe and receive a free copy of a booklet "**11 Steps to a Free Lifestyle**". For those of us who desire liberty and sustainability, this is an important resource to have alongside this book.

Contents

Introduction

Wow. Haters. What a topic. They are everywhere. But especially, they are on the internet, and are armed and ready to gun down your ambitions and your business dreams—unless you develop the proper psychological fortitude to hold your own against negativity.

I wanted to develop this booklet for a long time, primarily because I've seen how haters have ripped friends and business partners of mine *to shreds*. It's this phenomenon, perhaps tied to various other uncertainties, that keeps *countless* people from pursuing their business goals and living to their greatest potential.

This creates a kind of internet related *scopophobia*, or "fear of being seen". After one or two bouts with nasty people, or simply witnessing other friends experience it, the thoughts of putting oneself out amidst the sharks becomes terrifying. Potential artists, YouTube marketers, business-people and authors can all be affected badly enough to withdraw to their shells as proverbial turtles.

In this program, the tenth booklet of the *Cyrus Kirkpatrick Lifestyle Design* series, we are going to explore:

- The different ways doubt and negativity by others may be projected at you.
- The personality types that engage in this type of behavior, and why they do it.

- Drawing lines between constructive criticism that can be used to your advantage, and internet bullying.
- The proven strategies to ameliorate their threat to your morale and professional success.
- Exercises to help you glide past haters in your life.
- And quite a bit more.

As with all of my business related books, I try to remind readers about the *big picture* of the "lifestyle design series": leading a life of personal and professional freedom, doing what you *want* in life—never becoming a wage-slave, or otherwise a slave in any other respect in your life.

By now, you may have read some other guides about online business or marketing, but without a strategy to deal with the haters you could get stopped in your tracks the moment you upload what you thought was a perfect YouTube video to promote your work, only to receive six down-votes and some kid telling you to shoot yourself.

Or, it could be that unfair, scathing Yelp review by somebody with a questionable agenda.

Or, the nagging sensation imposed by certain friends and family who seek to discourage versus support your goals.

...Or, the aggressive attacks by the more malicious haters who directly seek to sabotage your professional aspirations.

Without creating a strategy for these types of people, your business and personal motivation levels will maintain a critical weak spot.

About the Author

My name is Cyrus and I run mobile businesses that are combinations of product development (semi-passive income) and services (including copywriting and editing). I graduated from the University of Arizona, I love to write books, and I also have a strong interest in filmmaking.

Since starting my business pursuits online, I quickly learned the value of ignoring other people's criticisms, opinions, or down-right attacks. It's inevitable, and it's always going to happen; whether it's because of jealousy, or any other topic outlined in this booklet.

I quickly learned that these psychological factors are as important as any other element in an entrepreneur's life. They can determine whether you get up in the morning and have a productive day, or you roll around in bed until noon, depressed and unmotivated.

Before We Get Started

If you liked this book then you don't have to be a stranger. While I get a dozen e-mails a day, I actually read and respond to all of them.

This usually leads to things like business opportunities, new friends, partnerships, and a chance for people to connect and receive help with other topics (I always answer questions and help with lifestyle topics for free). You can shoot me a line at cyrus@cyruskirkpatrick.com.

So, let's learn how to deal with haters.

Chapter One – On the Nature of Haters and the Internet

A hater, defined, is anybody who takes another person's work or business—and injects an unnecessarily critical slant to it. There are many reasons for why people do this; from a mistaken desire to help, on up to a purposeful attempt at causing damage.

The veracity of haters ranges from people who may actually have constructive feedback for you, children trying to get attention, family or friends with jealousy or attachment issues, on up to bitter enemies with a relentless axe to grind.

Haters comprise many categories. However, there's a clear distinction between two types: real-life haters, and the anonymous internet mud-slingers.

- In real life, haters are more often of the subversive variety, and the negativity is more of a subtle, manipulative nature, which we'll discuss in the next chapter.
- By contrast, on the internet, haters are generally much more outspoken, vocal and explicit.
- An exception are malicious haters, or the people with an agenda to harm you—who may become vocal opponents both online, and in real life.

According to studies at Elon University[1], anonymity is the factor that enhances cyber-bullying. Normal social conventions predicate that people behave a certain way, to enable reciprocity and to avoid social consequences like feelings of isolation, and to even prevent physical danger should the wrong person get pissed off. On the internet, haters are prevalent because these real-life concerns are no longer serious factors.

Further, psychologically speaking, it is very hard for a person who does not suffer from some type of sociopathic disorder to look a person in the eye and tell that person something negative and damaging unless it's absolutely warranted.

However, in an anonymous venue, it's possible for a person to enact the motions of anger or hatred without these consequences. For people suffering with anger issues, resentment, jealousy or any other type of bottled-up hostility, the internet allows them to pick fights in a "safe" venue—often with total strangers—where they can vent their frustrations or express their personal hostilities.

This manifests as a sliding scale between internet users becoming slightly more aggressive, to certain personality types who use every opportunity possible to lash out at their fellow human beings.

---

[1] https://www.elon.edu/docs/e-web/academics/communications/research/vol3no1/04DoneganEJSpring12.pdf

I've come to research that these are not the only factors that propagate the phenomenon of internet aggression. There's another factor that further tempts people to become aggressive, attention-seekers: and it's a neurological one.

Hating as an Addiction

For some, lashing out at strangers actually becomes an addiction, and there are common chemical enemies to blame.

According to some doctors and counselors[2], it's actually possible to become addicted to feelings like anger. Getting into a fight with somebody can be a huge boost of adrenaline and other brain chemicals, and while it's impractical and dangerous to seek out fights in real-life, the internet can become a conduit for this type of excitement.

The vernacular for this behavior is "trolling", which is when a person picks fights on the internet, sometimes randomly, to create this jolt to the pleasure centers.

Trolling may seem to be a sport whose demographics are just above grade school, and while certainly there are a lot of schoolyard bullies on the web, do not believe that this behavior always diminishes with age. The truth is that

---

[2] http://www.angermanagementresource.com/dealing-with-anger.html#sthash.5yobg9Ak.dpbs

anybody with a bit of inner-rage, and a seething addiction to cortisol and adrenaline, could turn him or herself into an anonymous bully.

Sometimes, in fact, it is those adults who hide behind their monitors who are the hardest to deal with. While a fifteen-year old telling you to shoot yourself because he did not like your YouTube video can be dismissed with a quick chuckle and a ban, the adults can be far more damaging.

An adult hater is more likely to be the person to write a long, detailed review that unfairly skewers you, using the appearance of intellect and logic to get under your skin. Or, it could be somebody that you think you're on familiar terms with, sharing ideas on a group or forum—only to find sudden hostility directed at you, and an effort to marginalize your work and reputation.

Both these subversive, assassination-oriented haters, and the shotgun-style, insult-throwing haters, have in common a persuasion to demean others for personal satisfaction; tapping into a very primal, addictive desire to pick fights and try to knock others down as part of a (usually illusionary) quest to reach the top.

Entering the Jungle

Given the prevalence of anonymous hatred, it goes without saying that attempting to fire-up any type of business or enterprise with an online presence is going to attract not just one or two critics—but *swarms* of people who independently, or sometimes in an organized fashion, will be committed to:

- Hurting your self-esteem.

- Hurting your reputation.

- Damaging your bottom line.

This will manifest as:

- Disparaging remarks on YouTube or other social media, sometimes to an extreme level, and usually masquerading as "criticism".

- Obvious smear attempts by "competitors", including hateful blog articles that misrepresent your services, and social media quarrels.

- Angry, typically unfair comments on your website's blog-roll.

- Angry e-mails.

The first, most important lesson to understand in regard to dealing with this type of hostility is that the battle is not you against the negativity; but your own mind against the influence of such people.

In other words, most of the times the determining factor for how much damage has been caused is how much you allow yourself to be affected.

The first important point to learn in this book is that **there are two traps** that people fall for. These are the reasons why so many people are badly affected by such behavior.

Trap Number One: Responding

The first immediate trap that so many fall into is the pattern of responding to negativity and fueling the ambitions of haters. **Without fail, the worst thing a person can do is engage the venom**.

The way such people effectively cultivate deceitful behavior is that they **fish for evidence based ammunition**. What this means is that the more information you provide to them, the more ways they can pick it apart and use it against you.

Ex.: Your video is amateur and poorly created. I have seen eight better videos in an hour of browsing YouTube. Truly, you are a hack—a two-bit wash-up. There is absolutely nothing redeemable about your channel, and you can pretty much fuck off and die.

Correct Response: Ban the person from your channel. If no option exists to do that, you can try starting another discussion or cultivating other comments to drown out the voice of the hater.

Bad Response: *Listen, buddy, I'm trying to make a living for myself, and you have no right to attack me without offering anything constructive (yadda, yadda)*

In life, in dealing with people—whether anonymously or face-to-face, a valuable lesson is that those people who thrive on negativity are truly fishing for responses. When you give such people more information, **they will use it against you.**

It can be hurtful to imagine that other people have such a negative prerogative, but understand that it's their battle to fight—not yours.

Trap Number Two: Listening

The second trap is modifying your behavior to suit the hater. This means you have taken what they've said to heart, or you've made the mistake of trying to spin their words in a "constructive" light as something you can use for your benefit.

This fulfills a common goal of the hater, which is to knock down / eliminate "competition" or anybody they feel does not deserve success. By listening to them, and taking their words seriously, you will stray from whatever your current course of action is and begin to adapt in some way that they desire.

Therefore, the only proper way to deal with haters involves both ignoring and forgetting whatever they've said. Admittedly, this is not easy to do. The empathic parts of ourselves take criticism harshly, because by default most people with healthy emotions will try and listen to and / or accommodate the voices around us.

While there are rarer instances when a hater is actually trying to provide something constructive and is not being as malicious as he or she sounds, the majority of the time it's not something that is worth investing energy into. Please see the next section on:

Understanding Constructive Versus Destructive Criticism

Criticism is derived from Latin criticus, or one who passes judgment, and always maintains overtones of "censurer" or "faultfinder"[3]. These days, thanks to the internet, nearly everybody is a critic. The challenge is finding when criticism is useful.

In the delicate world of dealing with people's emotions (including your own), criticism can range between being very helpful, and very offensive.

---

[3] http://www.etymonline.com/index.php?term=critic

As a type of "life skill", it generally pays off to be very receptive of critique, and to (by default) not view the majority of criticism as something that is harmful. In fact, most critics (who are not of the hater-variety) provide feedback for the purposes of being helpful.

In these cases, it is indeed "feedback". As a creative producer, if somebody points out something wrong with a video I've made, or a new book—this is extremely valuable to me because it means my reputation is being preserved and the quality of what I produce will be increased.

I feel this is something that's important to mention right now, very early, because I don't want people to go around misidentifying everybody who provides constructive criticism as being a "hater".

However, over-sensitive people make this mistake all the time, and it can create a lot of unnecessary stress and drama. We've all had experiences dealing with these types of people in workplaces—you generally feel as if you are walking on egg-shells around them.

By contrast, those people who are not very sensitive about their work—and view the value in criticism—are the people who we often feel the most comfortable sharing ideas with and (when necessary) pointing out mistakes or problems.

It's best for you to aim to be this type of person. Do not place excessive attachment on your work. The creative process involves constant revision, and other people's opinions can be a blessing and not a curse.

That being said, this mentally grounded, positive approach to criticism is also the best place to identify the differences between toxic and constructive critique. There truly is a "threshold" when advice and the constructive building process turns into something negative and hostile.

By identifying this "negativity threshold", it's easier to guard oneself against angry personalities. Furthermore, it keeps a strong defense against taking the wrong advice. Trying to extract constructive remarks out of a hate-filled e-mail or an angry comment is a fruitless effort. If anything useful can be construed, it's coming from the same wrongly calibrated mind of the person spewing venom—and it's unlikely anything productive can be gained.

The Motivations of Online Haters

A moment ago I mentioned the phenomenon of trolling and the likely chemical addictive nature of creating strong emotions. While this may be a subliminal causative factor, haters often have more surface-level motivations behind their comments to justify their behavior.

Some common factors that rouse the attention of angry personalities online include:

- A piece of media contains an overtone that could be interpreted as political in nature (that they disagree with).
- An artist's personal style (writing, filmmaking, etc) triggers a bias, bad memory, or a familiarity with something else that is disagreeable.
- A person feels he or she deserved a higher standard of information or service.
- The hater has a preconceived bias toward a person's racial or religious background.
- The hater is attempting to denigrate another person in an attempt to boost his or her status among peers (to "look cool").
- The hater is attempting to denigrate another person in an attempt to squash competition (the fake Yelp review by a competitor).
- The hater is a subversive type (see chapter two) and believes their opinions are for your own good will; while they are really trying to keep you confined to a box.

Most of these are overt or semi-overt motivations. In other words, the competitor who writes nasty and fake remarks on Yelp is unlikely to admit that he or she is engaging in unethical behavior; however, at the moment that they are performing the action, they feel justified in their behavior.

This is why it's hard to reason with such people. There's usually too much of a justification in their minds that their behavior is acceptable. Combined with what are very likely psychological and emotional disorders, then such arguments are impossible to win and futile to engage.

On Trolling

In my opinion, it's much easier to identify people whose sole intention is to spread mischief. The reason is because their arguments appear stretched and "fake" without any of the justifications listed prior. For instance, a so-called "troll" (internet instigator) may find a forum of people who celebrate a particular movie; and the troublemaker will lambaste the film in question simply to enjoy the ensuring outrage; but their arguments will not be particularly concise or interesting.

Feeding Trolls

In the world of internet lingo, you'll often hear people say "Do not feed the trolls!". Admittedly, when I first saw this phrase uttered, I was very confused and wondered if it was a reference to the ugly neon-haired "troll dolls" of the 1990s. Nowadays, however, "troll" is in the common vernacular, and feeding (or not feeding) trolls comes up in nearly any online discussion.

This is actually the commonly accepted psychological tactic to ignore an instigator's presence. If the motivation is simply to stir up trouble, they will get bored and wander off somewhere else if nobody feeds their craving.

Unfortunately, this rarely works a hundred percent on internet forums, because there's always one or two people who freak out at seeing their favorite movie bashed by someone. This is all it takes to keep the troll satisfied and laughing.

Is Trolling Harmless?

"Trolling" amounts to, in essence, schoolyard behavior made manifest online. Sometimes a "troll" is just a prankster. Somebody who is usually young, and looking for a bit of fun by poking at people's sensibilities.

I've been known, even as a full grown immature adult, to prank people if I get sufficiently bored enough by work. One time, I created a fake Facebook account claiming to be a space alien lizard-man, and I started pestering people from the conspiracy theory crowd who believe the royal family and other important people are reptile aliens (you can add me on Facebook, type in "Sarthak Reptilian").

A couple of people actually fell for my prank—people so embroiled in conspiracy theory books that they believed I may have been a real alien. The hilarity that ensued ended up going viral on Reddit.

So, I can't rag on trolls too badly if I am, in fact, a master troll myself. However there is a dividing line between pranking people online for fun, and becoming an actual internet bully.

Working online and doing a lot of work through social media, I've seen an endless amount of harmful, destructive behavior that overreaches "pranking". I've seen cancer patients mocked and girls with depression told to kill themselves.

This type of behavior is as awful on the internet as it is anywhere in real life. You can get involved with helping victims of this behavior at the End Cyber Bullying Organization (http://www.endcyberbullying.org/).

If you have children or loved ones with sensitive conditions who you wish to protect from malevolent behavior, advise them to stay away from certain online groups and communities.

In my opinion, this is the number one way to prevent being a victim of internet bullies. **In general, the less moderated a community is, and the younger the demographic, the more toxic it will be.**

It might seem harmless joining that huge, 50,000 member Facebook group, but it's definitely not a place to share personal information with anyone who has not been personally screened.

In the worst instances of bullying, a person's privacy will be invaded, and then the internet will be used as a means in which to disparage that person and / or even destroy that person's reputation.

This was the case for a young woman named "Rhoda Kelly"[4], whose boyfriend uploaded an unwarranted sex tape to a revenge porn website shortly after they broke up, and then further distributed it using the vindictively anonymous medium of 4chan.com. This resulted in an endless amount of harassment and psychological torment for Kelly (she was brave enough to share her story on the magazine site, Nerve.com).

In this case a real-life event triggered the horrible ordeal. This can occur in a variety of other situations, as well. For instance, rumors of a sickness or physical condition can spread among a school, and that school's social media circle may begin mercilessly shaming that person.

This type of bullying has always existed, but the internet has exacerbated it at a time when a few clicks of a mouse can send information to countless thousands of people.

To fight back against this behavior, remember to not affiliate yourself with toxic communities. A forum that is unmoderated enough to allow instances of this type of bullying should not be given the monetary support of participating in it.

---

[4] http://www.nerve.com/love-sex/true-stories/my-ex-posted-revenge-porn-photos-of-me

When Online Haters Actually Threaten Your Business

Given all of this information, when do these types of people pose an actual threat to your bottom line?

This can, in fact, happen when you are dealing with "internet saboteurs", the type of hater I mentioned previously who is attempting deliberately to attack a competitor's business.

I've seen this occur in hard to believe ways. As an Amazon self-publisher, you'd be surprised some of the viciousness out there. A couple of friends in my author groups have before been attacked by "trolls" who will methodically one star every book. Some rudimentary investigation then proves that the instigator is an author himself who is trying to knock down other people's work to gain more sales.

These types of assassination attempts also occur in the brick and mortar business world. The restaurant industry is filled with stories of warring cafes and bistros who will one-star each other's Yelp accounts, using fake profiles or even outsourcing the dirty deed to professional mud-slingers.

This is a very sorry state of affairs but it's no more than a reflection of human nature in general. The silver lining is that there's a type of natural karma in the world, and these types of tactics usually backfire.

Here are the basic strategies for dealing with these situations:

- **Compile Evidence:** Get to the Yelp or Amazon reviewer's history page and look for a pattern of behavior. If they're a new account with nothing but negative reviews of your products, this can be considered suspicious behavior.

- **Check for Lies:** More evidence can be used against the attacker if the review suggests they've never actually been to your restaurant, read your book, listened to your music or whatever the medium is.

- **Petition the Site:** On Yelp and Amazon it's possible to report abusive reviews. The harder part is convincing them that the review was that of a saboteur. Follow this link to get an updated Yelp customer service number: http://gethuman.com/phone-number/Yelp-com/, and this link for Amazon: http://gethuman.com/phone-number/Amazon-com/.

- **Get an Attorney:** If you can conclusively prove who is behind the attacks, you can file a defamation lawsuit.

- **Get an Investigator:** A PI might be able to help compile such proof. This can be worth it if you think the case is strong enough that the eventual lawsuit will recoup the legal and investigatory fees, and then some.

Chapter Summary

The anonymous nature of the internet is how many people with pent up anger, nefarious agendas, or cruel tendencies can express themselves in a very atrocious manner. It's important to immediately create boundaries, and to avoid the major pitfalls of 1.) responding to them and 2.) listening to their vitriol. In the case of saboteurs, there are steps to take to try and limit their damage.

On the same note, it's also important to be open to criticism. Not everybody are "trolls" or "haters", and very often negative feedback—especially noticing a trend of collectively bad feedback—is your key to improving whatever your talent is.

Very often, the people who get left behind in the professional world are the ones who don't listen to their customers and do not adapt to proper complaints. Sometimes we even see this in large companies who keep pushing out terrible products. For instance, Adam Sandler could certainly listen to some Rotten Tomatoes critics before he drops his next bomb.

Hey! Wait! Person reading this! Yes...You!

Do you have a copy yet of the free booklet that goes alongside this program?

It's called "**11 Steps to a Free Lifestyle**" and it's designed to help round out your education in a better lifestyle; with an emphasis on creating a life that's FREE.

This means less expenses, less worrying about other people telling you what to do, and being more INDEPENDENT.

Just go to www.cyruskirkpatrick.com/subscribe and enter your e-mail and I'll send it to you.

After you sign up, I'm also available to answer any questions you have. Like, I'll help you with problems you're having if you e-mail me with advice about your travel plans or online business ideas.

That's like, free consultation. I have way too much time on my hands.

Chapter 2 – The Subversive Hater

So far, we've talked about anonymous mud-slinging haters and internet jerks. In this chapter, we will talk about a much worse breed of hater; especially in regard to your personal aspirations and business plans: the subversive hater.

These manifest as people you know in real-life who project their limiting beliefs onto you. They pose a much greater risk because they're the ones most likely to penetrate your wall of skepticism and cause you to actually make serious decisions or doublethink your plans.

Subversive Hater Behavioral Traits

The following are ways that this type of behavior manifests. Take heed:

- A friend, family member or associate may appear non-receptive to your lifestyle, work or other goals. Or, they may feign interest and support…

- But slowly, such a person will attempt to influence you in a very different direction by inserting their opinions in harmful ways.

- They may say things like, "You know, there's a new report about how people who move to South America have a higher chance of being murdered," or "I hear 95% of startups fail and it's wiser to stay employed in a real company."

- At first this behavior may seem like concern, but the Subversive Hater will repeat these "concerns" in a way that may become more and more aggressive.

- Such a personality type is doubtlessly of the manipulative variety, and they may become agitated the more dead-set you are on your own life versus taking their "advice". As time goes, the passive behavior may turn more hostile.

- They may appear as overbearing family members, but they can also crop up as friends or even associates who, for whatever reason (jealousy, personality issues) take offense to your decisions.

The Psychology of Subversive Haters

The key component is passive aggressive behavior, which is the tendency to mask resentments behind behavioral changes and small jabs. According to an NYU Medical Center study[5]: a passive aggressive may appear to comply or act appropriately, but actually behaves negatively and

---

[5] http://www.psychologytoday.com/blog/communication-success/201401/how-spot-and-deal-passive-aggressive-people

passively resists others. This type of behavior also exists in the realm of the subconscious, and the perpetrator may not even be entirely aware of his or her actions.

A subversive hater, who is also passive aggressive by nature, is motivated typically by one or more of the following feelings:

- Jealousy
- A sense of personal inadequacy
- A fear of change
- Existential conflicts or a negative worldview
- A personal grudge or desire to see another person fail.

In most instances, the psychology is quite textbook. A person sees a peer trying something that does not fit the mold, and he or she feels a sudden sense of insecurity, given that they have invested time, money and emotions into a life that they have convinced themselves is the best choice.

This insecurity leads to an attempt to rationalize that their life choices are better than the other person's. Therefore, they feel the best solution is to block that person from living differently, by reminding them that the "status quo" is the best place to be.

This behavior is also common among emotional codependents.

Finally, the behavior may be solely the result of a narcissistic personality disorder. A person may believe their opinion and worth is over-exalted, and that they have literal power over other people's lives. As such, they may want to influence a person's life for the singular reason of having the opportunity to express that kind of control.

Therefore, it's important to understand that the subversive hater may not necessarily disagree with or dislike your idea, so much as they are expressing an ulterior motive of control.

Aggression or Concern?

Probably the most difficult thing about dealing with subversive haters is that they hide behind the guise of being concerned, or trying to help. The most dangerous of this personality type provides toxic advice that distracts you from your goals, while presenting it in such a way as to sound logical and convincing.

"But I care about you," is a common argument. However, what they really care about is their own insecurity that you'll leave them. This type of behavior is common among people with deep separation anxieties. For instance, a parent may tell their child that it's in their own best interest to attend college in the home city, despite their acceptance to an ivy-league school across the country, and they will not admit their selfish motives of being scared of loneliness or seeing their child leave.

A couple of things to note:

- Firstly, this behavior is common, especially in families. It's rather tragic when a family members uses manipulative tendencies, but it's virtually inescapable when there are strong emotions involved (and if that family member already has a tendency to manipulate to get his or her way).

- The most common tool that's used by this type of subversive behavior is guilt. They know it's hard to directly convince somebody logically, but by manifesting a sense of guilt or shame, a person may change their opinion on their own accord.

- This type of behavior typically starts on a small level. Therefore, it's easy to predict who in your life is going to act this way when you try to make a big decision. If your aunt has a tendency to guilt you into not buying her ice cream, you'd better believe when you try to move to another city she will pull out every trick imaginable.

Social Programming Parrots

Family members pressuring you is one concern; but among colleagues and friends, the more common way that your goals may be subversively thwarted is among what I call the "parrots".

A parrot is somebody who chronically thinks "inside the box" and the idea of doing anything outside of the straight-line of thinking is heretical. In other words, they parrot society's most common assumptions, and work hard to keep you inside that paradigm.

Here are some wonderful examples of parrots in action:

You: "I'm going to travel the world"
Parrot: "Great, so when you're back in two weeks, let's go have a beer" (parroting the idea that people never leave their home country for more than two weeks at a time, and that it would be irresponsible to do otherwise).

You: "I'm selling my car because I'm tired of spending thousands a year at sleazy auto repair shops"
Parrot: "You'll never be able to have a normal life again" (parroting the (American) idea that it's impossible to have a decent lifestyle on a bicycle, Vespa, scooter, or by foot)

You: "I'm going to pursue my dream of being a photographer even if it kills me."
Parrot: "I have a better idea. I hear *Geico Insurance* is hiring new employees." (Parroting the idea stable office jobs are the only path to success and that new entrepreneurs generally fail).

You: "I'm going to do my own thing until I'm successful"
Parrot: "It's better get in debt and be successful right now" (Parroting the idea that mortgages and car loans are

a good thing that brings you closer to what, in America, we call "The American Dream").

You: "I'm going to go volunteer in Africa"
Parrot: "You'll get ebola and die" (Parroting whatever fearful thing is on the news this time, but is grossly inaccurate for the majority of people).

You get the picture.

Unlike a social manipulator, most **parrots** simply don't know any better. They are the result of lifetimes of social conditioning and being taught to obey the rules. Social programming parrots also typically live their lives trying desperately to keep up with expectations from media, advertising, and false depictions of humanity.

In other words, they grow up watching *Everybody Loves Raymond* and believe that the proper template for a correct lifestyle involves: a suburban neighborhood of a big city with ready-to-go retirement homes when you get older, a husband who's kind of dumb but maintains as a breadwinner and loves sports, a wife who's clearly more competent than the husband and wears the shoes, children who inexplicably get along, and only first world problems to ever worry about.

I also meet social programming parrots at different age groups who maintain very specific ideas about living a proper life according to their demographic. In college, it was the "frat guys"—every other word that came out of their mouths was about "getting hammered or "blitzed" or "faded" last night.

That's because in college, you drink a lot, try to hook up a lot, drink some more, party a lot, and sometimes study. Again, social reinforcement in action.

The danger of this type of behavior, whether you are dealing with them or you are in fact a parrot, is that real life is about **constantly changing dynamics**. A lifestyle of peer reinforcement is fickle when everything can change at a moment's notice.

The college party girl / guy with no life skills whatsoever is going to be in a serious predicament if he or she has to suddenly perform CPR on someone, or try to counsel a friend who is about to kill himself.

The person who gets the mortgage and the lofty career as a sports writer is going to be in for trouble when the business model of that magazine falls apart when a hipper online competitor appears on the scene.

In *Everybody Loves Raymond* (I don't why I have such a bone to pick with that show, but I do) there was never an episode where Raymond successfully created a fall back career and small business with his egotistical wife, unless it would involve Raymond totally fucking up the entire process because of his tendency to be goofy in all the wrong areas.

The successful people are the ones who constantly evaluate their lives and approach patterns of stability with skepticism. Instead, they plan around the long-term issues of not only finances, but emotional concerns. At age 30, they can see over the horizon to age 40 and think "Wow, unless I do X, Y, Z right now, I'm going to have one hell of a mid-life crisis in ten years."

They're also more likely to take risks that could endanger their social standing, something that is again quite heretical for a social programming parrot. Giving everything up to go make a movie might not be financially sound, but there's plenty of long term benefits emotionally (accomplishing goals) and even professionally (being recognized as a self-starter, opening doors to VIP places).

To deal with parrots, you should be willing to ease them out of your life if they can never accept outside of the box thinking. Most decent people relax and let others do their own thing, but occasionally somebody may come out of the woodwork who becomes downright offended by your subversive behavior, and they will more aggressively try to fit you back in the box.

If that happens, cut and run; try not to keep such people around in your life, if they don't naturally go in a different direction anyway. Never get caught up trying to conform to society's expectations that are represented by the champions of the status quo.

Prejudices and Biases

Another huge factor to influence a "social parrot", or any hater in your circle of family or friends, are cultural biases.

It's a shame to think that in the 21st century there are still racist agendas even in our own communities, but I've seen it time and time again. I remember growing up in the deserts around Arizona, I'd never seen a single black person in our community. One time, a neighbor in his 20s bemoaned that he was forced to work with a "nigger" at his new job.

This can be very problematic if these types of people are in your community, and you are trying to do something to upset the status quo.

Depending on the severity, I'd suggest to cut and run and *get out of there as quickly as possible*. Being an educated person means that you have greater opportunities for both riches and happiness in your life. There is no way to intermingle these types of prejudices with any type of high quality lifestyle.

Prejudices like these are basically negative emotional feedback circles. That little twinge of pleasure to denigrate another person or lifestyle, and build up oneself, is what creates the addictive quality of such behavior.

You don't need to be on that plane of consciousness. You can find better pleasures in much healthier ways. And, associating yourself by geographically being around such people will—whether you like it or not—begin to influence your behavior and eventually make you start to act like them.

A Battle of Willpower

Whether or not you succumb to another person's attempt at influencing you largely depends on your willpower and desire to see your own goals through to completion.

I've always been amazed by how few people really accomplish things they want to do. At the first sign of resistance by friends and family, they buckle and it's over.

But in some ways, I can understand this. My own parents, God bless them as they are getting older and are not in great mental or physical health, have tried every trick you can think of to keep me from leaving my home city and doing my own things in life.

This is because of emotional reasons. I'm the youngest in my family, and at some point I was designated with the title of "emotional glue" to keep everyone together. I hate to rag on my own family in an e-book that will be likely read by thousands of people, but I'll go ahead and spill the beans: there's no shortage of things like crises, baggage and alcoholism in my family.

Because of my tendency to think logically and always keep my head on straight, I performed my job well of keeping everything glued together back in my home city. Major crisis? Well, I can drive over and handle it. Money disappearing faster than it can be made? Well I'm great with computers and ideas, so I can think up of solutions. Someone is morbidly depressed? Well, I always think of the best life advice (not that anyone ever implemented it).

It was like this for far too many years. So, as you can imagine, the pressure was laid on THICK for me to stay in my city and seek "stability", as by proxy certain people in my life could also feel more stabilized—with me acting as a center of gravity.

I remember watching "The Shawshank Redemption" and likening myself to Andy Dufresne with his very long escape plan.

My situation, however, was not that different from a lot of people I've known. As a result of my own life experiences, it's become easy to identify other people who become emotional hostages due to people subversively hating on their ambitions.

And certainly if I had had less willpower, I would have never started pursuing the lofty goals that I currently seek. There would have been no extended trips abroad, crazy jobs doing things like writing and travel journalism, or very long stints of business creation, which all became hallmarks of my 20s.

I feel very satisfied and without regrets because of my life, as I've led it up until now, has involved mostly doing what I've desired to do. However, if I had continued to try and serve people in my family, this would have never happened.

I think it's important to understand that it's OK to be "selfish" in the sense that you're developing yourself to the point where you can more concisely help people that you care about in the future. This is probably the best way to eliminate guilt. If you're around overbearing personalities, they WILL invade your personal goals and boundaries. This hurts your finances, happiness, and breeds resentment that will only hurt your relationships with these people.

Doing your own thing, on the other hand, means you're leading your life according to what's important to YOU, and it puts you in the optimal position to perform a practical step in the future—such as making a boatload of money and helping your parents retire.

Finally, I've noticed that people with emotional codependency issues typically *require* the time apart to ever be able to grow. Some will scream and whine, but they'll adapt and become better as a result.

In addition, your "parrot" friends may require seeing somebody break the mold to discover for themselves that going outside of the box is actually a viable option. They'll exist as critics up until they see that it works, then they'll join your bandwagon and ask you constantly how you did it.

Cutting Past the BS

One way that I deal with these types of people is that I point out exactly why they are criticizing my work or feel afraid of my success. This is a great way to cut into their subconscious and semi-subconscious and demonstrate that you know what's up.

Ex.: *"Starting your own photography business sounds great, but there's so many good jobs available in your home town. You won't have to worry about paying rent by doing something that you know works."*

Response: *"I understand you're afraid that if I do this, you won't see me anymore or it might be a reflection of your own inadequacy if I succeed. Don't worry, I promise you that my own path is very much related to my own unique goals and ambitions and it's only for the best of everyone, including yourself."*

Resist the urge to argue after this point. Some may get offended, especially if you've just struck a cord and shined a light on behavior that they'd rather not admit to. Let them deny it all they want, you've made your point clear and you don't have to continue the conversation or further listen to that person.

Resisting Hesitancy And Taking a Big Step

If you find yourself succumbing to the criticism / negative influence, and you are caught in-between taking the necessary actions and over-thinking the alternatives, then lean on the side of what you really want to do, and take one big step toward accomplishing it.

For an example, if your dream job is in Los Angeles, buy a plane ticket to Los Angeles. A non-refundable one, preferably.

Now, you've just invested money into your goal and there's no turning back. The chorus of criticism will amplify at this point, and the subversive haters will likely switch gears to become more aggressive in their ambition to keep you chained down.

From here, it's kind of like the mask is taken off and it becomes clear that their motives are more self-serving than anything else. It becomes a lot easier to strive forward with confidence when it's clear you've made a decision, and when their arguments begin to fall apart.

Should You Cut Ties?

This is a hard but commonly asked question in regard to subversive haters. When is it time to completely cut such people out of your life?

Obviously, the answer with family is not to do it. There's no sense in creating a permanent rift because of a disagreement of priorities. And, I've seen these rifts occur. Once more to reference my own family, both of my parents were essentially black sheep themselves for going off the grid and not living up to my grandparent's expectations.

Not surprisingly, history began to repeat itself. However, I've made it a point not to drop off the face of the Earth. I care enough about my family to routinely visit and even financially support them if it came down to it, but I must focus on my own goals as the only way to get to that point.

Cutting ties is only a viable option if, despite that you are keeping strong boundaries, the situation only appears to be getting more and more toxic. Examples include heavy alcoholism, physical or heavy emotional abuse, or any type of danger to your welfare.

"Nagging" or disagreements are not an excuse to disappear from the lives of former friends and family. However, serious dark situations may warrant such actions.

Chapter Summary

Subversive haters are often those among friends and family who have ulterior motives to see that you maintain shackled to your current way of life. As a result, they will create convincing logical or guilt-infused arguments to keep you from doing what you want to do.

It's important to remember that their criticisms have motives. Sometimes, they'll even create the appearance of being constructive, as this is the best way to convince a person or to make them second-guess their choices.

I know first-hand through my experiences that it takes a lot of mental fortitude to resist this influence. And, just about 99% of the time, it's in the best interest of EVERYBODY that you pursue your own goals instead of trying to live up to their expectations.

If possible, avoid long drawn-out arguments with these people. It won't do any good, it will just create a rift that could last years.

Chapter 3 – The Malicious Hater

While the subversive hater may have convinced him or herself that your best interests are in mind, the malicious hater is the personality type who is aggressively out to make war.

They appear online, in the media, as a competitor's business (as explained in chapter 1 with the saboteur Yelp reviewers), or in the form of a personal enemy who has decided to bring up old wounds and try to destroy you as part of some elaborate revenge plot.

The latter category may include exes, people you've fired, the mentally unstable, or perhaps someone you've legitimately wronged in your life (you slept with their significant other)—you've never made amends, and now that person feels all they have left in life is the quest to destroy you.

Let's elaborate a bit more on these different types of malicious haters, and how best to deal with them:

The Professional Tool

Whether literary or movie criticism, there's a lot of people trying to up their careers as "professional haters". Strongly disagreeing with something, even arbitrarily, or trying to pick a bone with some up-and-coming artist is an excellent way for a self-described critic or literary review genius to stand apart from others.

This is something that artists of various mediums, writers, and designers have to deal with. And, once you begin experiencing a modicum of success, the "professional tools" will come out of the woodwork.

This can be a very debilitating process for anybody who is trying to build up their career. And, it's basically inevitable.

Examples:

A blogger destroys a new painter who was just accepted into a popular gallery. An up-and-coming movie critic finds your indie piece at a festival, and rips it to shreds. A reviewer on Amazon blasts your novel you finally finished with one star (but is sure to include a link to their literary critique blog at the end of their attack).

The important distinction about a "professional tool" is that their sole purpose is, really, to bury people. In other words, the actual quality of your work is of no relevance. So, it would not matter whether what you created was good or truly awful, these types are interested only in criticism as a way to prop up a sense of intellectual superiority, or to impress other critics in similar fields.

So what do you do in these situations?

"The Any Publicity is Good Publicity" Approach

How deeply criticism affects buying and viewing habits is arguable. Lately, summer after summer, we've seen movies that have received the lowest marks possible by critics exceed all expectations at the box office (the "Transformers" movies, "Teenage Mutant Ninja Turtles" and countless more).

That being said, sometimes the best approach is to ignore the criticism and remind oneself that even negative publicity is a symptom that not only people are paying attention to your work, but people are taking it seriously enough to feel it needs to be attacked. Very often negative criticism is a sign of your work becoming more popular, therefore you will get more viewers, customers and so forth.

And this is because, in general, whatever it is that you're creating—maybe it's music, or film or art or a physical product in the sense of business—will resonate with the people it's supposed to resonate to. And, it's not likely that one person's bad opinion will make much of a difference because those people who are resonating appropriately will not find it agreeable to even listen to that person.

The only time there's a real problem is if your work is not resonating with *anybody* and therefore your art, or your products, are not being viewed or purchased at all, and the little bit of reviews you receive are negative. In this case, it might be time to listen to your "haters" and work to create a higher quality product.

Going on the Offensive

Some choose to go on the attack against unfair professional criticism. This can be a dangerous path to walk because it can give an artist the reputation of being a "cry baby". In Hollywood, there are famous stories of director Uwe Boll challenging his critics to things like boxing matches (where Uwe, a professional boxer himself, generally wins). Needless to say, this has not aided his reputation.

There might be a few occasions, however, to respond to or even attack the critics without tarnishing your own professional reputation.

- If the critic blatantly gets facts or information about the work wrong.
- If the critic makes a defaming allegation, such as accusing the creator of stealing someone else's work.
- If the critic has created a reputation of mud-slinging, works for a competitor, and it can be proven.

A one-time response, in these situations, may be a good idea. Usually critics have the so-called moral high-ground, but if unethical behavior is being engaged in, it's possible to rescue one's reputation and turn the tables back on the critic.

The Vendetta Keeper

Another type of "malicious hater" is the person who has a vendetta against you, and your work. Some things to keep in mind:

- There is sometimes no logical explanation behind it. The vendetta is caused by some emotion outside of your control. It manifests by a person hating everything you do.

- The person with the vendetta is in a weaker position socially because he or she, instead of masking as a genuine critic, is concerned with directly attacking and ruining a person's reputation, which appears less genuine to outsiders who may just see it as someone with a bone to pick.

- This may also include people with mental and emotional problems, who for whatever reason are expressing their rage against the world—and you're the hapless bystander.

- It is also very often someone you've legitimately wronged, and they are now trying to destroy you. A good motivation to keep practicing that Golden Rule at any rate.

I've heard some nasty tales of people's ex-lovers and other enemies going out of their way to ruin everything a person does. In life, one's professional reputation can be a fickle thing, and this is why such attackers at the very least believe they have so much sway and power.

Here are examples I've personally seen (but thankfully seldom experienced):

- **The Attack Blog:** I've seen ex, disgruntled employees create attack websites to go after their former bosses. The idea is to get it to the front of the Google listing, so that anybody who Googles Bill Lumberg (or whoever the bosses' name is) immediately gets a lot more information than they were anticipating, including sordid personal details.

- **The Product Horror Story:** Just how bad of a victim mentality can one person create from a product they didn't like? Sure, sometimes it's justified, but for everybody who was legitimately hurt by a product or service, there are six more people who are just seeking sympathy and a way to vent anger. This manifests as attack blogs, anti-product social media campaigns, and even formal petitions against the creator.

- **The Deceitful Defamation:** I've seen exes get people fired. There are infinite varieties of revenge that people plot in this way, and the idea is to lie about the victim in a believable fashion. They may hire someone to plant false allegations and then make complaints to an employer. They may also try to ruin the victim's future relationships by

- **The Honest Defamation:** Again, often among ex friends, lovers or associates who know each other's details and weaknesses. This type of attack is far more damaging because it's built on facts instead of lies, so it's much harder to refute. Examples include any situation of unearthing dirt from someone's past, and making it very well-known.

The Psycho

While the Vendetta Keeper may be justified if only in a perverse sense, there are no shortage of psychos in the world who may come after you without any rationalization that could be inferred by a normal person's standpoint.

In my experience, this is more common as one gains a higher amount of popularity or attention. You better believe celebrities deal with psycho stalkers and haters on a near daily basis. This is why somebody like Jessica Alba travels with a militia of bodyguards and security.

As soon as a person enters the spotlight, it's an inevitability that some person with severe emotional problems is going to latch on to the image of that person, and start taking things further and further, perhaps blaming the public figure for not responding to longwinded letters. That obsession will turn into a representation of the instigator's own self-loathing—in other words, rage.

Psychos can be best handled with law enforcement. They are less crafty, less slippery, and less manipulative—they are like a blunt instrument. However, they can still be dangerous. A malicious stalker can engage in any of the reputation destroying behavior of any other type of hater, with the added bonus of being totally irrational.

The Career Assassin

The career assassin is a very deadly type of malicious hater, because he or she will deliver the most heinous techniques imaginable to destroy someone—not because it's personal, but to eliminate someone from a position in a job that the instigator desires.

In some ways, this is the worst of all the archetypes I've listed. Professional tools are just annoyances, vendetta keepers suffer from human flaws, and psycho's require psychiatric care. The career assassin, however, is calculated in his or her destructive qualities, and may suffer from some type of sociopathic personality disorder (in essence, the inability to experience empathy).

They appear almost entirely within careers where the very ambitious strive to the top. The career assassin is the journalist who sabotages a co-worker's report to incorrectly cite a source or fabricate a quote, or it's the actress who has the tires of her rival's car punctured the day of the big audition.

They may also engage in more trivial matters. As mentioned back in chapter one, a version of the Career Assassin is the business owner nextdoor who hires saboteurs to one-star your service on Yelp, or it's the rival author or product seller who gets on Amazon to drop your rating.

As you can imagine then, there's a gradient between petty behavior, on up to the worst crimes imaginable (murdering someone to get their job or remove competition). However, I would not be surprised if someone willing to perform the most petty of actions would not eventually stretch their morality thin enough to consider the worst.

The assassins are the most manipulative and clever at all. If you think you've found a way to defend yourself or fight back—think again, they've rehearsed every possible scenario in their heads to be one step ahead of the game.

However, this doesn't mean that this type of person wins in the end. Their Machiavellian approach to life may be a source of pride, but in a tic-for-tac world where giving always returns more than attacking, these types usually obtain only short-term success. Sometimes, if their sociopathic tendencies dimmer as they age, they may look at the horrible karma they've reaped and experience irreparable nervous breakdowns by age 40.

When People Make War, What Do You Do?

Despite even the best attempts by the world's greatest conflict avoider, it's inevitable for things to go sour with people, and to eventually get a malicious hater in your midst.

Here are some ideas to keep in mind. The focus is on preparation and a solid defense:

Identify: Consider who among your professional or social circle might be imbalanced enough to freak out on you or try to destroy you. This isn't being paranoid, it's being defensive as you must around the wrong types of people.

An example might be that co-worker who appears mentally unhinged, makes strange remarks toward you, and seems somewhat obsessed with what you do. Such a person has red flags all over.

Or, it could be your current significant other who you're on the verge of breaking up with, but that person has a long terrifying history of going on vindictive spirals of destruction and revenge against unsuspecting targets for sometimes petty reasons ("That person double parked near my parking space? Help me get some sand to put in his gasoline tank."). You better damn well believe there's going to be some fallout when you get away from such a person.

Prepare: Keep a digital voice recorder with a nice, solid battery life on you at all times, and make sure it's positioned in such a way, whether in your pocket or taped to your shirt, that you can actually hear dialogue on it and not just your T shirt moving back and forth.

If you're in routine communication with the potential crazy person, when things later get ugly, it might be really helpful (especially for legal reasons) to have the instigator declaring something to the effect "I'm going to destroy you!".

Boundaries: Before anything gets to Defcon levels, make sure your boundaries are in place and that you use them alongside your effort to identify problem people before they become actual problems.

This means do not constantly be a provider of information about your work life or personal life, unless you've been able to very clearly judge the person's character. In general, the two worst people to divulge information to are the potential malicious haters, and the gossipers who malicious people can later pry for details.

Defensive Posturing: Next, try to create a preemptive battle plan. First, judge where you are the most vulnerable. If, for instance, it's your relationship with your boss, try to strengthen that relationship, and if possible—

depending on the context of the threat you are diagnosing—you may be able to let them know in advance that you are dealing with some unhinged personalities. It's a hard topic to bring up while not seeming like a drama monger yourself, but it may be necessary if you clearly see a train coming down the tracks.

In addition, make sure you have proper insurance in place. If, for instance, you provide a service that has any type of risk involved, ensure your liability insurance is active. A malicious person may be just waiting for the perfect opportunity to exploit a weakness in your business and then use it to position some type of lawsuit against you.

If you're concerned the threat could pose a physical danger, be ready to file a restraining order and / or get away from their physical proximity—stay at a friend's house, anything.

Finally, look for a free consultation with a good attorney, and at least get the confidence of having his or her phone number in your purse or wallet.

Assess Damage, Fight Back: Not everybody who's "out to get you" is really going to cause that much harm. Likely, an angry ex who writes to your boss and claims you're a child molester is going to be considered a crazy person, and it's not going to cause any real harm.

But obviously, these situations can also turn ugly very fast, and create endless problems for you. This is when it's important to figure out how much damage is being caused, and whether it's necessary to take steps such as suing for defamation of character, or in the case of the extreme examples: getting law enforcement help.

Clean Up Mess: If you're a well-branded professional, it's because of these situations that the public relations career exists in the first place. An instigator understands that how someone is perceived is often based on subliminal and psychological factors.

For instance, the famous trick in political battles is when a faux journalist asks a competitor politician "How would you respond to allegations of pedophilia?" A hypothetical question, but by the act of "denying" non-existent pedophilia charges, voters identify that politician with a very bad thing—even if the link is totally made up.

Public relations is about then changing that dynamic back in favor of something that you want. One example might be to appear on the news doing something charitable or positive, that gets people's minds off whatever "scandal" you had been sucked into.

The idea is to rebrand yourself and pivot in a direction that's completely different from whatever incident may have drawn negative publicity.

Ponder Situation, Take Responsibility: However it is that you ended up in a situation where you were at war with someone—it would be very wise to take a step back and consider how you ended up there in the first place.

Although you're not responsible if a crazy ex tries to ruin your career, you may be responsible for a long term pattern of behavior if you find that you consistently get emotionally involved with the wrong types of people. If you have a long and predictable pattern of these things happen, you may ultimately be the source of your own problems.

Another example could be repeat incidences of former employees who want to destroy you. Yes, one or two were off their rockers, but what's the message that's coming back to you? It could be either that you're hiring process is totally off base, bringing in the wrong types of people—or you are legitimately mistreating your workers.

Here are two case studies, based on everything we've learned so far, that might help you figure out these situations better:

Case Study: Chipotle

What types of situations could create large amounts of enemies for you, in a short amount of time? I can think of at least one:

A Penn. State Chipotle (a Mexican restaurant franchise) likely created more than a few enemies for its owner. In September 2014, the restaurant suddenly closed down (see pic at this link: http://i.imgur.com/zBGi45F.jpg), with a sign posted on the front door: "Ask our corporate offices why their employees are forced to work in borderline sweatshop conditions. Almost the entire management and crew have resigned."

At the Reddit page for the incident (http://www.reddit.com/r/pics/comments/2g0k2g/apparently_chipotle_isnt_a_good_employer/), a former worker at that specific restaurant describes conditions where new employees were expected to learn months of skills, without training, on the first day, with many more issues that went far worse. Overall, restaurant service jobs are hard, but everyone seemed to agree this one particular franchise was above and beyond way worse than it should have been.

If you're running an operation, what is the culture and has it become toxic like this infamous Chipotle franchise? If so, you put yourself at risk of: lawsuits, people who want to ruin your career, and a lot more types of enemies.

Keep track of people who work for you, and people who work for other people who still answer to you. You may be a perfectly nice person, but if you've created a monster—you're going to take the heat, and you may end up in very sticky situations.

Case Study: Bryan Singer

In early 2014, the entertainment world was shaken up by allegations against X-Men director Bryan Singer by an individual named Michael Egan who claimed Singer had sexually molested him during a string of infamous Hollywood party-slash-orgies. Egan filed lawsuits against several other entertainment executives, as well.

In late August 2014, Egan dropped the charges. In fairness, it does not exonerate Singer as a suspect, as it's more indicative that Egan ran out of money to be able to keep such a lawsuit active, but it does illustrate how the simple act of being attacked and charged with something can place a person in a compromised position.

Singer, who in all likelihood is innocent, was still subject to comparisons to the stories of former child-star Corey Feldman, who also claimed abuse during pedophilic Hollywood orgies, and this brought further suspicion on him in the eyes of the media. Despite Egan dropping the charges, it's hard for the image of Singer to remain completely untainted by the scandal.

Assuming the charges were unfounded, this is an example of a malicious personality; namely either the vendetta keeper or the psychopath, hell-bent on destroying someone by hitting him in the most societally taboo way possible. And, as a public figure, Singer's best defense was ultimately a world-class public relations team, who are undoubtedly still working hard to clean up the aftermath.

It also showed how malicious personalities choose to go after their targets. In this case, Singer was just about to release *X-Men, Days of Future Past*, which was a major highlight of his career. Most analysts of the situation did not find it coincidental that this is when Egan became poised to attack, as it was carefully chosen based on when he could do the most amount of damage possible.

Chapter Summary:

The malicious hater, unlike the subversive hater, is anybody who desires the destruction of an opponent's career, reputation or livelihood. This is not merely trying to discourage a person from achieving their goals, but it's a direct attack.

The motivations range from people attempting to exact revenge (who may, in fact, even be "justified"), to psychopaths with delusions of grandeur. It may also include people trying to boost their own careers, from the tools who fabricate reviews and attack budding artists, to the more clever and dangerous career assassins who take this several steps further and orchestrate destructive attacks on rivals in the most sociopathic ways possible.

In human society, we have to stay aware of such people, and create our own personal public relations and damage control strategies when such incidents inevitably happen. In the vast majority of cases, unhinged personalities cannot harm your livelihood in any long-term fashion, however in cases like with Bryan Singer, an attacker with a well thought out strategy can be very costly indeed.

Chapter 4 – Clearing Out Negative Influence

In this chapter, we'll discuss how to avoid cultivating "haters" in your life, and strategies for dealing with the negative influence of both people who want to directly sabotage you—and people within your family or social circle who incorrectly believe they're doing you a favor.

Why Negativity Sticks

Psychologically, there's a tendency to place greater weight on the negative. We don't count our blessings so much as we count the ways things could go wrong. We rarely call our friends and tell them about the good news, but we will definitely call if our fear switches get activated by some totally inconsequential threat of terrorists, or bears, or some serial killer a thousand miles away.

This is a good, natural tendency because fear overrides the status quo. This keeps us alive and aware of our surroundings. In short, negative emotions trump positive ones.

However, our circuitry to pay attention to negativity is supposed to be short-lasting. It's not supposed to be a person's entire life. The status quo is meant to be the default—which is, a sense of safety and general peace as one lives their life. The jarring feelings of fear and conflict are considered to be unusual circumstances that occur once in a while—but are dealt with, and then normality and reason returns.

Our high stress lifestyles, however, seem to condition us to respond to—and live amidst—high stress, negativity oriented lifestyles full-time. We may spend our entire day being at the receiving end of angry drivers, clients, bosses, etc—and then it's only natural that our cortisone enriched days end with freaking out about parents pressuring us and exes stalking us.

So, what do you do about this?

Lowering Stress, Cultivating Happier People

As I talk about again and again in other books in the "Lifestyle Design" series, probably the first thing to do is get your priorities straight. As Arianna Huffington (founder of the Huffington Post) argues, there is a third metric besides wealth and power—and it's lifestyle happiness.

If that third metric is out of alignment, then you can try to amass wealth and power all you want, but you won't be happy and you'll be cultivating unhappy people in your life.

Also, here's a bit of a revelation: **the more generally unhappy and stressed out you are, the more "haters" have an emotional impact on you**. It's a phenomenon where one negative occurrence compounds with the next, and when after an already unnecessarily hard day you get some freak on Yelp yelling at you because some sandwich you sold him gave him gas, it's easy to reach the "breaking point" and start throwing furniture against walls.

Here are some ideas to put into action:

- Get rid of clients who are very high stress. The money you lose is worth the peace of mind almost always.

- Finish work at set deadlines and avoid "bringing work home". If your office is high stress, don't spend your free time pacing around the house thinking about the next day's problems. Socialize or do something very different from your job in your spare time.

- Consider a change of career if your lifestyle is irreparable (I'd suggest the first book in the series, "How to Quit Your Job", for this).

- Don't put all your eggs in one basket. Criticism or insufferably angry haters of any fashion outlined in this book have far more power over someone who has pinned their entire career and ambitions on one or two projects.

- In other words, don't write one album as your magnum opus, try releasing a few different albums. Or, be known for a couple of different aspects of your career.

- Don't feel you're trying to rise to the top against all odds, with nothing to stand in your way—because sometimes this type of drive can come back to harm you. Inevitably, trying to be one step more driven and ferocious than the next person will draw "Career Assassins" discussed in the prior chapter into your life—who will see you as a threat because you're playing the game on their level.

- Spend a day—or a week—accepting being "wrong" about things. Another reason negative people may be targeting you is because you're too rigid in your points of view. This can threaten other people who are equally rigid, and lead to nothing but drama.

Haters Versus Givers

Next, it's important to identify the opposite of a hater or a de-motivator—which is a "giver"—somebody who zaps others with positive energy, good-will, and support. In other words, any charismatic person that people enjoy being around.

Here are some traits of "givers" that most reasonable people can agree are very pleasant:

- Recognizes their own needs in contrast to other people's.

- Cultivator of positive emotions in social settings—seeks to constantly build other people up in both small ways (a smile and a greeting) and large ways (emotional support and helpfulness).

- Unaffected by emotional dependencies—willing to allow people space to be themselves.

- Emotionally honest—will not try to mask ulterior motives behind logical reasoning. In other words, if a family member moves, won't try to convince that person to stay based on logical premises when the real reasons are selfish.

- Handles conflict concisely and through being open and honest. Won't plot to slash someone's tires.

- Avoids passive aggressive behavior and grudge holding. Either lets it go or resolves it.

- More interested in happiness, creativity, fun and relaxation than resentment, anger, hostility or grudges. Therefore, seeks to ameliorate the latter and prop up the former.

- Places more value on lifestyle and happiness than appearing better than peers—and is therefore less likely to betray values or ethics to get ahead in a professional world.

Now, you need to consider how many givers you know versus haters (or potential haters). Ask yourself if you're giving the haters in life more power than they deserve—power that should be going to the positive energy givers, instead.

What I've found again and again, using that tried and true Pareto 80/20 method, is that about 20% of the people in my life account for 80% or more of my fear / worry / anxiety. In reality, this is probably closer to 90/10.

For instance, people read my books on Kindle and often e-mail me. Literally 90-95% of my e-mails are positive, and 5-10% are "lukewarm"—maybe people questioning some of my theories. Approximately 1% of my e-mails are hate letters.

So, which e-mails do I pay the most attention to? Obviously not the fan letters, but the very rare instances when somebody writes me something to the effect of, "YOUR BOOKS SUCK, YOUR WEBSITE SUCKS, AND YOU LOOK LIKE THAT REDHEADED KID FROM THE HARRY POTTER SERIES".

So, surprise surprise, all of my energy for that week goes into dealing with this one person. "First of all, I'm not a redhead…" I'll start to write, only to stop myself moments later when I remember Trap Number One outlined back in the first chapter—responding to haters.

The issue goes back, once again, to our fear response mechanisms. The positive energy coming from the regular happy people—the good emotion "givers", is considered the status quo—the way things should be. It's the one dissident that poses a problem, and humans are, after-all, master problem solvers, and we feel the urge to fix that one problem created by the one dissenter. This brings me to a very important lesson:

Haters Are Not Your Problem to Fix

While part of our inclination to respond and stress out about these people is to salvage our egos, another big reason is because we are trying to "fix" a problem—that for whatever reason, this person is unhappy. As if we must make everyone conform like the Borg from Star Trek, we feel the need to assimilate them back into the happy space.

But it will never work because a hater is almost always waging a war against him or herself, not you.

Ultimately, the proper response is to always **cultivate more givers, and seek to be one yourself**. Close out of the window, ignore the threats, turn off the panic button, **and go seek people who appreciate your company**. Do not give the haters anymore energy than they deserve.

This is harder to do among friends and family, and other subversive haters. Except just keep in mind that while you may be obligated to be loyal to people close to you, you are not obligated to mesh with their ideologies and ambitions.

Without question, what YOU desire in life is going to be the proper path. What other people want you to do is by definition a reflection of their own selfish traits. There's no reason to hate these people or judge them for their human flaws, just try to stay the emotionally mature one. Disagree, be loving and supportive, but keep disagreeing. If you become a broken record—so be it, but don't fold.

One of the biggest causes of animosity among families that I've seen is when someone finally does "fold", and perhaps a son gives up his budding career as a musician to go work as an accountant—and then he hates his father for the rest of his life for ruining the chance he had when he was younger.

So, again, never fold—unless you want to cultivate long term damage and harsh feelings.

Where Are These Haters Coming From?

Lastly, let's consider how you might be bringing in the negative influence.

Although anybody can be a victim of an attack, there is a tendency for "like to attract like". According to psychologists, a person with a tendency to be conflict oriented may have some minor level of narcissistic or borderline personality disorder[6]. As a result, such a person is likely to bring in much more "drama" and negativity than others.

Is it possible that you may have some underlying condition like this? Give it a serious thought.

In diagnosing why you deal with so many haters in your life, don't rule out the possibility that your actions are very conflict oriented: including body language, tone, attitude and demeanor. This could be creating conditions that allow these types of people to foster; much like adding protein to a petri dish.

There is no magic bullet to cure any type of psychological condition; except to try and lead a life more considerate toward others. Think about doing things like adding value and spreading positivity wherever you go. The positive feedback that you'll return will, in its own way, become an addictive process. And it's much better to desire those pleasurable, positive feelings versus the cortisol and stress hormones that get released when you're fighting with someone or adopting a victim mentality.

And, if necessary, it may be time to learn whatever childhood factors precipitate a conflict attitude by setting

---

[6] http://www.psychologytoday.com/blog/stop-walking-eggshells/201205/high-conflict-people-drive-disputes-home-school-work

up an appointment with a psychiatrist and maybe getting into your rainy-day fund to pay for it.

Final Thoughts

Hopefully, this book has helped to expand your awareness in dealing with one of the final big challenges that an entrepreneur must deal with—the vocal, negative opinions of other people.

In truth, haters will never go away. No matter who you are and what you're trying to do, you will get people telling you that you'll never make it, that you shouldn't try it, that you should play it safe, and / or that you should go to hell.

Building the emotional callouses needed to deal with these types of people and situations is the hidden business skill that is 100% necessary to achieving any type of personal success and financial liberty.

At the end of the day, seek to emulate the go-getters who never give negative influences more than a second's thought. And, most importantly, believe in yourself. Do not allow the negative perspectives to make you regret the inevitable sacrifices that we all have to sometimes make to be able to make the most of our short lives on Earth.

Where to Go Next

Firstly, please let me know what you thought of this book by leaving me a review. Typically I release second versions of my books, and feedback allows me to make corrections and eventually create more enhanced editions.

Just head to the Amazon review page off your digital downloads list, and let me know what you thought.

Next, I invite you to navigate to the following address: http://www.amazon.com/Cyrus-Kirkpatrick/e/B00LYIV33K/ to view my Amazon author page. Here you can find the rest of the books in the **Cyrus Kirkpatrick Lifestyle Design** series, including titles that are designed to compliment this one, such as:

How to Quit Your Job
How to Make Money While Traveling
Freedom: How to Make Money From Your Dreams and Ambitions
How to Make a Business When You're Broke.
How to Actually Make Money Blogging
How to Escape the Rat Race and Move to Beautiful Countries
Kick Ass at Viral Marketing
And **25 Terrifying Reasons Your Website is Not Successful**

Finally, the best way to stay in touch with me is through my mailing list. I'll provide weekly tips for your business, announcements about free books, and even a complimentary e-book about reducing your expenses and living with more freedom.

You can join at http://www.cyruskirkpatrick.com/subscribe.

I'll see you next time.

~ Cyrus.

Made in United States
North Haven, CT
20 January 2024

47665903R10043